WHY SHOULD I EAT THIS?

Let's Talk About SUGAR

TABLE OF CONTENTS

By Lindsay Snea

A Crabtree Seedlings Book

Crabtree Publishing

crabtreebooks.com

School-to-Home Support for Caregivers and Teachers

This book helps children grow by letting them practice reading. Here are a few guiding questions to help the reader with building his or her comprehension skills. Possible answers appear here in red.

Before Reading:

- What do I think this book is about?
    - *I think this book is about food.*
    - *I think this book is about sugar.*
- What do I want to learn about sugar?
    - *I want to learn which sugars are better to eat.*
    - *I want to learn what foods contain sugar.*

During Reading:

- I wonder why...
    - *I wonder why sodas and candy have added sugar.*
      I wonder why eating too much added sugar can make us sick over time.
- What have I learned so far?
    - *I have learned that natural sugars are found in fruits and vegetables.*
    - *I have learned that some foods have sugars added to them.*

After Reading:

- What details did I learn about sugar?
    - *I have learned that we should brush our teeth one hour after eating a sugary snack.*
    - *I have learned that it is important to make healthy choices about the sugars we eat.*
- Read the book again and look for the vocabulary words.
    - *I see the word **carbohydrate** on page 3, and the word **nutrients** on page 8. The other glossary words are found on pages 22 and 23.*

Let's Talk About SUGAR

Sugar is a **carbohydrate** found in many foods and drinks.

Carbohydrates give your body **energy** to play, to learn, and to grow.

Foods that have **natural** sugars include fruits, vegetables, and dairy products such as milk.

Foods with natural sugars also have **vitamins** and other important **nutrients** that keep your body healthy.

Sometimes **refined** sugars are added to make foods sweeter. Foods with added sugars do not have any of the nutrients that help you grow up to be healthy and strong.

DID YOU KNOW?

Foods with added sugars include sodas, cookies, candy, and ice cream.

Eating too many foods with added sugars is an unhealthy choice for your body.

DID YOU KNOW?

Sugar is also bad for your teeth. Brush your teeth about one hour after eating a sugary snack.

Too much added sugar is bad for your brain, heart, and bones. When you eat a lot of sugary foods, your body stores the extra carbohydrates as fat.

Eating too many foods with added sugars can make you sick over time.

Instead of eating foods with added sugars, eat foods with natural sugars instead. Choose berries or bananas, sweet potatoes or carrots, or a glass of milk.

It is important to make healthy choices about the sugars that you eat.

Glossary

carbohydrate (kahr-boh-HAHY-dreyt): A substance found in certain foods that gives your body energy

energy (EN-er-jee): Your body or mind's ability to be active or do work

natural (NACH-er-uhl): Not having any extra substances or chemicals added

nutrients (NOO-tree-uhnts): Substances that your body needs to live and grow

refined (ri-FAHYND): changed from its original form

vitamins (VAHY-tuh-mins): Nutrients found in foods that help your body grow and stay healthy

Index

About the Author

Lindsay Snea lives in the mountains of Fernie, British Columbia, Canada, with her husband and four children. Lindsay is an elementary school teacher, and a lifelong learner, who is passionate about cooking, food, fitness, being outdoors, and health.

Written by: Lindsay Snea
Designed by: Margaret Salter
Proofreader: Melissa Boyce
Photographs: All images from Shutterstock
Production manager: Candice Campbell

Crabtree Publishing

crabtreebooks.com 800-387-7650

In Canada: We acknowledge the financial support of the Government of Canada through the Canada Book Fund for our publishing activities.

Printed in the U.S.A./CP112025

Published in Canada
Crabtree Publishing
616 Welland Avenue
St. Catharines, Ontario
L2M 5V6

Published in the United States
Crabtree Publishing
347 Fifth Avenue
Suite 1402-145
New York, New York, 10016

Library and Archives Canada Cataloguing in Publication
Available at Library and Archives Canada

Library of Congress Cataloging-in-Publication Data
Available at the Library of Congress

Hardcover: 978-1-0398-8119-8
Paperback: 978-1-0398-8480-9
Ebook (pdf): 978-1-0398-8239-3
Epub: 978-1-0398-8359-8
Read-Along: 978-1-0398-8564-6
Audio: 978-1-0398-8522-6